BEFORE
YOU MOVE TO
NIGERIA

LOLA OJ

To Perri

Thank You x x Lola OJ

1

BEFORE YOU MOVE TO NIGERIA

Published in Nigeria
LOLA OJ LIMITED
22, Issac Aluko Olokun Street,
Igbo-Efon, Lekki Epe Expressway,
Lagos Nigeria.
books@lolaoj.com

Printed by:
MRL Productions
www.mrl.ng

DISCLAIMER

Although I am a lawyer, I am not your lawyer lol. Reading this book does not create an attorney-client relationship between us.

This book and the content provided herein are for general information, educational and entertainment purposes only. This book should not be used as a substitute for the advice of a competent attorney admitted or authorised to practice in your jurisdiction if you should need one.

The character in this book 'Titi' and other characters mentioned in reference to her story are entirely fictional, any resemblance to actual persons, living or dead or actual events are purely coincidental.

Every effort has been made to ensure that the content provided in this book is accurate and helpful to the readers at the time of publishing. However, this is not an exhaustive treatment of the subjects.

The author has made great effort to ensure the accuracy of the information provided in this book at the time of publication, while we try and keep the information up to date and correct, there are no representations, warranties, either expressed or implied about the accuracy, reliability or availability to the information, products of services contained in this book for any purpose.

Any use of this information is at your own discretion and the author does not assume and hereby disclaims any liability to any parts of the loss, damage or disruption caused by errors or omissions due to the information provided, whether such errors result from negligence, accident or other causes.

No guarantees of success are intended by this book, results may vary as no individual is the same. If you wish to apply ideas from this book, you are taking full responsibility for your choices and results.

DEDICATION

I dedicate this book to my mother, thank you for always supporting me.

PRAISE REPORT

I moved back to Lagos about half a year before Lola did and goodness it was a rollercoaster, although it definitely did help having someone else to share my woes with. I can say that I wish we both had a book like this to read before we relocated, it would have helped us navigate this new terrain better. If you are a returnee or intending returnees, do yourself a favour and read this book, it'll help you a lot.

Stephanie Coker Aderinokun,
TV host, Actor and Entrepreneur

I have lived in Nigeria my whole life so I do not have a relocation story, however, I do have many friends who come to me for relocation advice. Now, I can simply tell them to read this book! Relocating to anywhere can be overwhelming, relocating to Nigeria can be very overwhelming and this book gives practical tips to make it easy. As an author myself, I truly appreciate this body of work and I encourage even those who haven't relocated to read it as it offers a different perspective to what living in Nigeria can feel like.

Atewo Laolu-Ogunniyi,
Relationship coach & Author

I have known Lola for quite a number of years now and I have always been inspired by her focus, determination and drive. When I moved back to Nigeria it was her advice that helped me navigate the country and helped me navigate the cultures and traditions. Moving back to Nigeria was a decision that many people understood at the time when I moved but Lola saw a vision ahead and followed it, her moving back to Nigeria influenced my own decision as I was able to see a different side of Nigeria through her experiences, her tenacity is what I admire most, her advice motivated me and I am so glad she's sharing many of our experiences, good and bad, to show the reality of relocating to Nigeria.

Hannah Olatunji,
Marketing Executive and Entrepreneur

I have lived in London, UK my whole life but I frequently visit Nigeria and actually schooled there in part. I have often toyed with the idea of moving back to Nigeria and reading this book has highlighted some of the reasons why it may not be an ideal choice for me right now. As exciting as new beginnings can be there are important things to consider with the hope of maximising your results, I particularly enjoyed chapter 1 "Beyond the glam of Lagos" as I do think it is important to speak about the realities of permanently relocating to a new environment, thankfully Lola doesn't shy away from this and is very honest. There's a lot to gain from this book whether you intend to relocate or not, you will appreciate the honest and balanced perspectives.

Atinuke Olukoga,
Senior Associate, FinTech

How I wish I would have read this book before I moved! This is a realistic and unbiased account on what it is like relocating to Nigeria, there are some things that I overlooked before I moved and this book covers it, how I wish it was written sooner. Lagos, in particular is a very fast-paced environment and can take lots of adjusting, though very fun it can serve as a major distraction and thankfully this book gives you tips on how to navigate that when it happens. I enjoyed the honesty and also the jokes, very relatable.

I relocated to Nigeria for 3 years, relocating was an eye opening experience and though I'm now back in the U.K, I do not regret it. You never know where life will take you, I could find my way back to Nigeria again.

Well done Lola, it's refreshing to see someone share their experiences in the hope that it'll help another.

Nicola Olayinka,
Project Manager

TABLE OF CONTENT

FOREWORD

Migration is a huge undertaking that affects many aspects of a returnee's life. Perhaps, because I went through the process myself, I am fascinated and honoured to write the foreword of this book. At every stage of your life, there is a choice of where to live and for many reasons many Nigerians in diaspora choose to return to Nigeria annually. The paradox of migration in our time is most manifest in the fact that while some desperately seek greener pastures abroad, others, particularly Millennials and Generation Z who were born and bred abroad prefer to return to "the very place our parents left in search of greener pastures" abroad, as the author puts it. For whatever reason, if you consider returning back to Nigeria, Lola OJ provides a comprehensive compass of clarity of purpose in making informed decisions to why, how, what and when to return, as well as pragmatic insights on career goals, financial plans and general safety considerations.

For those born abroad, returning to Nigeria for holidays could be fun. But this isn't exactly the case for those seriously considering returning to settle down in Nigeria. In most cases, returnees are guided by myths emanating either from the media or from family members and friends about the challenges of living in Nigeria. No literature clearly gives you a clear-cut clue of the cost and price of moving back and productively settling down in Nigeria. In this *gist-like* narrative, the author settles your mind with what Nigeria really looks like – from the surreal fun that Lagos buzzing nightlife offers to the busyness of the daily business and commercial activities, she simplifies the resilience, hustle and fun spirit of Nigeria.

Beyond the lines of excitement that the idea of returning back home brings, you need to understand the Nigerian system, how to fit in and navigate the culture shocks that may affect you emotionally, mentally, socially and financially. Nigeria holds limitless lines of opportunities for you if you follow the resourceful tips this book presents which demystify the assumption that "things don't work out well in Nigeria". The spirit of hustle in Nigeria is the general rule that things work out well in Nigeria if you work hard and make the most of your experience. Just like any other country, so many things may not work according to your plans but the experiences shared in this book will "equip you to make smarter and wiser decisions".

And hey, don't worry, while you work hard, you will always have a taste of the Nigerian buzzing moments of fun – the parties, concerts, *owanbes* and even "champagne popping at Quilox" never ends. It is a culture that rewards our hard work and pursuit of exceptional enterprise as a people and society.

And though you may be far away from Nigeria, you have a civic role to play within your constitutional rights as a citizen in Diaspora, one of which is to vote during elections. Though diaspora voting is not yet recognized within our electoral process, you can apply for your PVC, schedule a visit to collect same and vote during elections. Getting your PVC to be part of the electoral process should be the first on your bucket list because the quality of leaders we elect will influence your enjoyment of a functional system upon your eventual return to Nigeria.

I feel compelled by the electrifying lines of this work to recommend it to anyone who is seriously desirous of returning and settling down in Nigeria for any purpose. I commend Lola OJ for enriching our migration experience literature at a moment when many young people are returning back to Nigeria to contribute to the socio-economic, cultural and political development of our country through their ideas, creative enterprise and innovations, particularly in the tech and entertainment ecosystem.

See you in Nigeria.

Hon. Dr. Shina Peller,
Member, Federal House of Representatives

INTRODUCTION

I was born and raised in London, United Kingdom in a typical British environment, however, the moment I entered the four walls of my home I was teleported back into Nigeria!

My father, even after spending a huge part of his life in the UK, is a very typical Ibadan man, complete with the mannerisms and dance moves. My mother, a very hard working and vibrant Ijebu indigen, raised me in the ways of my culture. It's not unusual to meet someone with such a mix, someone who is swallowing amala to the sounds of apala music one minute and naturally switching to enjoy fish and chips coupled with sarcastic British humour the next minute.

So you can imagine my shock when people in Nigeria would call me 'Britico' or 'oyinbo', I thought I was a typical Nigerian! Someone who willingly and joyfully enjoyed her culture was quite easily judged as someone 'not knowing their roots' due to my prominent accent. This of course, couldn't be further from the truth, I LOVE being Nigerian! I visited Nigeria for the first time in my teens, little did I know that that first encounter would begin my journey into discovering this new world!

Some years passed and I plucked up the courage to relocate back to Nigeria, it was an exciting yet anxious time, would I like it? Would I survive? Would I be embraced?

I learnt a lot along the way, made a lot of avoidable mistakes, but managed to progress and achieve in various ways. When I would meet people based abroad like I once was, they would ask me, how did you do it? I honestly didn't feel qualified to give advice since after all in my mind 'I hadn't made it yet'. I would meet a group of people again and they would say, 'you're doing so well, how did you do it'? On a trip to London, I sat down, faced my iphone towards my face, used my parents lamp and and decided to answer some questions people had about my relocation. That video, although very low budget, gained traction and more questions kept coming in, so I decided that I would compile some useful tips, things I wish I had been told before moving to Nigeria.

I sincerely hope this helps, it was written based on my experiences and experiences of returnees around me. The things you ought to consider before relocating permanently, the things I wish others would have told me.

BEFORE YOU MOVE TO NIGERIA

Chapter 1

BEYOND THE GLAM AND FUN OF LAGOS

Her bags were packed and her ticket bought. In a few days, Titi was going to land in Lagos. It had been almost two decades since she lived in Nigeria. Although she had made several trips back home for the holidays, this trip was going to be different.

Her parents were nervous. They had sacrificed a lot to give her and her siblings a better life in the United States, so they did not understand why their daughter was making this move to a country they had deliberately left behind. There were all kinds of stories about how hard life was in Nigeria. So, like any average parent, they worried.

That did not sway Titi one bit; she wanted to do something different with her life. She had made up her mind; besides, she was convinced that Nigeria is where she was meant to be for the next stage of her life. From the trips she had made over the years, Lagos seemed like a city filled with opportunities. In addition, she had enjoyed her holidays with family and friends in Lagos, which was one more thing she looked forward to upon her return—time with friends and family.

***

Every year, Nigerians in the diaspora choose to return to Nigeria. Some have to return because their visas have expired; others just choose to relocate back home, like Titi in the story above.

In my case, I was born and bred in the UK, and before my big decision to relocate, I had only been to Nigeria twice. Like most immigrants, my family relocated from Nigeria to the UK to give us a better life, which begs the question: Why do so many young people decide to return?

Why are Millennials and Generation Z choosing to return to the very place our parents left in search of greener pastures?

Ironically, I grew up hearing and seeing a lot about the challenges of living in Nigeria. In my mind, I can still picture the images I saw on TV—military men clad in khaki and kitted with armour as they paraded the dusty streets.

As a child, I couldn't picture anything beyond what I saw or heard. I had seen pictures of the country on the news. Some were pictures my dad took in Ibadan, and they were all I had to form my opinion of Nigeria.

I came to associate Nigeria with dusty roads and violence, thinking, as some Africans in the diaspora still believe till date, that Nigeria is a war zone. I did not know better because, unlike what we have today, there was no social media to correct that notion. All we had were traditional means of spreading information, like newspapers, pictures, television, and radio. Thanks to my first visit, I started seeing how unfounded the myths I had come to believe were.

The first time I came to Nigeria was for my cousin's wedding. In contrast to the image I had in my head, Nigeria was colourful, not misty and dusty, and no military men were parading the streets. I soon discovered that a phase of unrest, which the country was going through, had necessitated the presence of military men on the streets.

It is important to clarify here that there are numerous misconceptions about Nigeria and Africa that can serve as a mental block for returnees who wish to visit or relocate back home. You will hear so much misinformation that might serve as a deterrent. What matters, ultimately, is that you are making an objective assessment.

Being an IJGB (I Just Got Back), I had a lot of fun. My cousins were available to drive me around town. We visited so many places that I didn't know existed in Lagos. At the time, I was in my late teens and had restrictions on where I could go. Despite that, I enjoyed every moment I spent in Lagos. People warmed up to me and made every effort to make me feel comfortable.

Coming to Nigeria for a wedding was a different level of fun for me, and typical of the *Owanbe* party that characterises Lagos, the grandeur felt like I was clothed in Joseph's coat. The colourful traditional cuisines, attires, and smiles radiating on people's faces were the direct inverse of what I had expected. The music was different from what I was used to, yet my body seemed to understand how to sway to its rhythm.

Owanbes are a highlight for any returnee—for any Lagosian, as a matter of fact. Literally translated to mean *it is there, owanbe* connotes the abundance of fun, food, drinks, celebration. You name it. It is an extravaganza of colours, the tallest *geles* (head ties), music, and paparazzi. A lavish party Nigerians throw, usually on weekends, to celebrate momentous events like weddings, birthdays, buying a house, and even deaths. *Owanbes* are best experienced.

But Lagos is not only about *owanbes*.

While revelling in the ecstasy of the parties I was attending, I asked my parents why they had been hiding Lagos from me, and their response was a knowing one: 'It is fun because you came for a wedding.'

When I returned to London, I couldn't stop ranting about my best holiday experience to my friends. I felt like I belonged when I was in Lagos. It felt like home, and I did not feel like a minority there. Despite the excitement, I forgot the experience once I adjusted to my daily routine in the UK.

Years later, I joined crowds of Nigerians in the diaspora coming home for the December holiday. This time, my experiences opened me to another layer of Nigerian holiday fun called *Detty December*. I was now past my teens and had no restrictions, unlike the first time I visited the country.

Detty December is not a myth; it is real. The buzzing nightlife in Lagos is real! I had a taste of it—from beach parties and hangouts to concerts, *owanbes* and champagne popping at Quilox (a popular club in Lagos). There was always a party to show up at. I attended as much as I could during my short stay.

However, things felt different when I returned to London. This time, I could not settle into my routine as quickly as I had done the first time. In fact, I got tired of the monotony of my life. I would wake up every morning, get on the train, go to work, and work from 9 am till 5 pm. It felt too static and boring. I wanted something new, something unlike what I was used to.

My elder sister was living in America, so I considered moving there. At the same time, I couldn't help but consider what moving back to Nigeria would be like. The more I thought about it, the less appealing America became. I believed that if I moved to America, it would be no different from life in the UK. Alternatively, Nigeria seemed like a good option.

I was a beauty enthusiast who had a desire to run a brand that produces eyelashes. When I weighed my prospects, I realised that the Nigerian market was perfect for my brand, and I stood a chance if I could successfully penetrate the Nigerian market. After deciding to expand to Nigeria, I made a few calls and contacted a PR Manager. We talked about strategies to publicise the business even before my arrival.

It wasn't long before I discovered a noticeable difference between holidaying and living in Nigeria. Many who have made the giant leap to move back to Nigeria are hit in the face with this reality.

I failed to realise that the buzzing nightlife I saw while holidaying was only possible with the busyness of the day. Lagosians may be having fun at night, but they utilise their day well—something a returnee might be oblivious to.

***

It had been a few months since Titi's return to Lagos. The illusion of what life would be was slowly unveiling, making way for the reality that life in Lagos is not the dream she had expected.

The first thing Titi noticed was that people barely had time for her during the week. They were busy living their lives. The second thing she noticed was how bad the power supply and internet services were. During her visits prior, she had not felt the impact of both because family and friends had gone out of their way to make her feel comfortable. Now, she was no longer a guest. She was now a resident of Lagos city.

Still, she tried to cling to some semblance of her life in America. She needed some comfort in this strange place. To compensate, she ate at fancy restaurants that served meals she was beginning to miss, but it was starting to take its toll on her purse.

***

Nigeria might seem fun to people who have experienced the merriment of the holiday season, but the fun is not a good enough reason to make the big move back home. Like Titi in the story above, returnees sometimes do not think too deeply about the cost of moving back home.

The purpose of this book is to provide clarity for those thinking of moving back to Nigeria. Having clarity about how things are, will equip you to make smarter and wiser decisions about your move. The truth is that you need to consider your reasons for moving. It will be best if you do not make your decision based on friends who have made a move, or on what you see on social media.

What you see from afar is not always the same when you come close. If you are going to make this journey, you need to have a legitimate reason for moving back because when it gets tough, your reason is what will keep you there.

Every day is not a holiday. You need to have this at the back of your mind.

Another challenge many people overlook in their excitement is the culture shock they will face as they try to navigate living in Nigeria. After the first few weeks of returning, it will become clear that you might have different values and beliefs compared to those around you. Living in Lagos can be stressful for an average Nigerian and much more for those who have lived away for so long. Therefore, besides ensuring your financial capability, you need to think of your emotional and mental health as well.

Before making the big move, I had it in mind that every day wasn't going to be *Detty December*, so I prioritised my business. In hindsight, however, I had made some errors because I did not fully consider certain things before returning. I had not stayed in Nigeria prior, so my plans at the time were based on what I heard from family and friends.

My decision to move back was accompanied by so many yeses and noes. People discouraged me, and with good reason sometimes. Leaving my family was the hardest because I had to give them a reason why I wanted to stay back. My parents left Nigeria because they wanted to give us a better life, so telling them I wanted to go back to the place they left, without a logical explanation, was not an option. Eventually, I told them that I wanted to serve my fatherland, and my dad, being the patriot that he is, agreed to it. Years later, I did serve my fatherland through the National Youth Service Corps (NYSC) program.

When you think of moving back, think long-term. Make plans, and don't get distracted by what you think you might meet because the reality can be a lot different. Money doesn't grow on trees in Nigeria; you will work hard as you do abroad. The fun in Lagos is real, so also is the hustle. Likewise, do not be deceived into thinking that things don't work out well in Nigeria. It is a false assumption.

If you don't understand the system, you can't fit in because you will frantically exhaust time, energy, and resources without yielding the right result. Therefore, I'll advise you to prepare as much as you can. There is a big gap between preparing and preparing well. I thought I had prepared well, and in a sense, I did. I had a place to stay; I had a business to start—which, in the long run, would take care of my finances, and it did—but that was not enough.

There was more.

BEFORE YOU MOVE TO NIGERIA

Chapter 2

'CHOP LIFE' SYNDROME

Before Titi relocated to Nigeria, her parents ensured that she had enough money to cater to her needs till she was financially stable. They were sceptical about her decision to move, but her mind was made up. They also insisted that she stay with her aunt and not hesitate to reach out to them if she needed anything.

After Titi arrived in Lagos, she started applying for jobs. She knew that she needed a stable income to survive and could not depend on her purse for long. Though her saved-up funds and her parent's consistent financial support could last her for a while, she still needed a stable income.

Three months later, she was invited for a job interview at a reputable firm. After undergoing several stages of the interview, she was offered the role of an auditor with good pay and mouth-watering allowances. The job offer was a huge relief to her purse, and with her savings, she could worry less about her finances.

Surprisingly, six months later, Titi found that her purse had depleted, and she didn't know what had gone wrong. The money she had saved up was completely exhausted and what was left was barely enough to sustain her through that month.

***

Relocating is a big undertaking that affects many aspects of one's life. It can be exciting, but it is necessary to think about finances and make adequate plans before making the big move. Frankly speaking, we often believe our financial plans are airtight because we have money saved up in our accounts; as such, we feel relaxed.

The last thing you want to experience as a returnee is being stranded, and this can happen if you fail to plan your finances.

Don't make the mistake of thinking that financial freedom is dependent on savings. It isn't. No matter the amount you've saved up, you will eventually run out of it. That's why, along with your savings strategy, you need to have a financial plan that summarises how you manage your money, or better still you need to just have a budget.

Not everyone likes budgeting, and that's with the wrong assumption that budgeting means a restriction on spending. If this is your perspective of budgeting, maybe the word 'budgeting' is off-putting to you, then let's call it a 'spending plan'. The purpose of this is to help control your spending, track your expenses, and save more money.

Just like you have several reasons why you need to budget as a returnee, there are several ways to budget. You can track your expenses and allocate your resources well by hand, with a pen and paper. Or, if you want to do as little work as possible, use an app. The key game is to stick to it, though it might be tough. If you give it a fair try and can't find a way to make it work, jump ship to another method that will have a tremendous impact on your finances.

I'll advise prospective returnees to make better financial decisions. If you're planning on moving back home anytime soon, you need to have a long-term financial goal that you need to start planning towards now, and not when you move back home.

Before drafting out your budget, ask yourself to assess your priorities. What will my needs be back home? How much do I need to earn, to comfortably cater to my needs, as I make the big move back? What percentage of my earnings do I need to set aside to cater to contingencies?

Don't expect your budget to be perfect. Some expenses may slip through the crack, but you can take precautions by setting aside a little bit of cash for miscellaneous expenses. The accommodation you thought was less than 500 thousand naira may increase in price when you arrive. Inflation is one constant factor in Nigeria's economy, so be prepared. It is one of the powerful elements that threaten to take away what we've worked for.

Money management can be a difficult task, especially without a stable income. It goes beyond spending less than you have or being prudent. A true sign of financial freedom is having more than enough with which you can live comfortably. Therefore, you need to get your financial house in order if you want to avoid catastrophe.

Your determination to attain financial freedom should drive you to pursue a stable means of income. For others, it may be having enough money saved to manage unexpected events so you can sleep well at night. I don't want you to be that person who doesn't have enough money to stay afloat, and becomes dependent on family to subsidise spending.

Financial freedom is building wealth and security. The income can flow in through a job or a business. Either way, before you get your first salary or your first client, you need to think about how you will survive.

Those first few months are important, and they come with bouts of frustration. You don't need to add money problems to the list again. So, take care of your finances.

***

Since I had a business plan in place before my move, I began to market my product, *Blinx Lashes,* soon after my return. The market was not as saturated as it is today, so it was relatively easy to make headway within a few months. In hindsight, things could have been worse if I had been faced with opposing factors. Thankfully, I was not.

Blinx Lashes grew impressively, and I started to earn from it in no time, but I know this is not everyone's experience. Some people move back with well-laid plans about businesses that go nowhere, which is why I like to tell returnees to have a deep financial reserve before returning home.

When moving into a new environment, there are a lot of things you cannot predict. At best, you can only trust that your plans will work out, but anything can disrupt those plans. The government can decide to implement a policy that makes it hard for you to do business; anything can happen, so you need to secure a means of financial sustenance for at least a year. Assuming that, at the worst, you don't have cash flowing in for as long as a year, you need to have something to fall back on.

I have to say, though, having a cash reserve is not a fool-proof way to scale the financial demands of moving back, even though it is the first step. Financial freedom for returnees is, very often, a process. As such, you need to decide early enough if you want to get a job or start a business.

While your savings will sustain you through your first few months, it is only a matter of time before bills empty it. The way I see it, earning is one side of the coin and spending is the other side. If you want to secure a balanced system around your finances, you need to earn. In my case, even after *Blinx Lashes* started making profit, I could not afford to get a place of my own. Still, it gave me something to save until I was able to afford a decent apartment.

When you earn, the additional income gives you leeway to afford the things you want.

After you have secured a way to earn, look for opportunities to invest. In their haste to earn, returnees often focus on earning and are left surprised when they end up broke. It is as much a financial rule as much as it is a rule for returnees; you need to invest your money, more so in an inflated economy like Nigeria.

Money is a tool; nothing more, nothing less. It's just like an app on your phone; if you don't use it right, it won't bring you the desired result. So, it's not how much money you earn but what you do with the money that matters.

I learnt this the hard way as I failed to reinvest because the rate at which money flowed in was the same rate at which it flowed out. I was pretty much spending as much as I was earning, leaving little room for much left, so this is something you want to watch out for when you return. You want to make sure you're not spending as much as you're earning, but have tangible investment at the end of the day.

My advice, as you plan your return is to look into investment opportunities now, preferably in a stronger currency. Nigeria is a breeding ground for so many opportunities; take advantage of them while you can. Don't think you can depend on your earnings or family alone.

***

Returnees often make the mistake of living the lifestyle they were accustomed to abroad without putting structures in place to accommodate the reality of the present environment. This is where the *chop life* syndrome can be of disadvantage. Take dining out, for instance. Dining out is a norm for returnees, and many times they don't mind the cost of a great meal.

I took that almost literally because, during my first few months back, fancy restaurants became like my kitchen. I normalised it to the extent that I was spending an average of ten thousand naira daily on food, oblivious to the huge red flag it raised in my finances. If I knew better, I would have opted for the affordable option of a *bukateria*, but it wasn't an option for me; it didn't have the appeal of a fancy restaurant, so I didn't consider it. When my purse started growing leaner, I didn't need anyone to persuade me to stop. I became a fan of *bukaterias*. I also realised that they are much tastier than I had thought.

Spending money on fancy restaurants, I just believed I was giving myself a fulfilling culinary experience, which I enjoyed countless times in the UK, so I understand returnees who spend money on a fancy meal. They're not thinking about going broke; they just want to enjoy a good meal in a decent restaurant as they've always done.

This *chop life syndrome* plagues most returnees, so they are tempted to enjoy themselves the same way they did when they visited over the holidays. They want to spend money the way they did before they moved, and they forget that moving back can be financially demanding. I am not opposed to *chopping life*, especially as someone who did so myself. What I am opposed to is doing so at the expense of sustaining yourself in your new environment.

***

Sticking to a restrictive budget can be suffocating, finding your way through investment jargon can be quite confusing, and many returnees often fall off the financial bandwagon despite their good intentions.

Looking back at my financial decisions, I made so many mistakes as a returnee. But over time, I have learnt from my mistakes, which I don't want you to make. It is better to be prepared than to be thrown into the wild and find out the hard way.

Don't get discouraged while in the process. Truly, attaining financial freedom is all a process; you don't get to the peak overnight; it is a conscious and gradual effort.

I know many people want to attain financial freedom, not just returnees, and sometimes they think working more jobs will get them there, but it does not. Even the highest paid jobs can plunge you into debt if you don't plan your finances well.

BEFORE YOU MOVE TO NIGERIA

Chapter 3

MIND YOUR LANGUAGE

Titi had recently moved to her apartment in Surulere. She had started adjusting to the new environment with the help of her neighbours who had been friendly and very helpful. Relocating from the United States to Nigeria was a huge step for her, and settling down was a big relief.

One fateful Tuesday morning, Titi woke up late for her usual morning jog. As she hurriedly descended the stairs, she bumped into her older neighbour, apologising in haste as she turned to leave. But her neighbour wasn't having it.

'Couldn't you look at where you were going'? The woman was visibly irritated. 'What if I fell and broke my neck or I slipped and got injured'?

Titi turned and smiled. 'Come on, that's silly. You are only exaggerating. Also, it wasn't intentional. By the way, I already apologised.'

Her neighbour watched in shock as Titi jogged away without a care in the world.

The following day, Titi greeted her neighbour and received a cold shoulder in return. Though she was taken aback, she had to leave for her office.

Later that day, Titi narrated the situation to her friend and colleague, Yemi.

'I think you were wrong; you shouldn't have addressed an older person using the phrase, 'come on, don't be silly', Yemi replied.

'Really?' Titi had confusion etched on her face. 'Back in the States, words like that mean nothing and people don't take it personally'.

Yemi chuckled before answering. 'Look here, my friend, this is Nigeria, not the United States. Words like that are interpreted as insults. I understand you are a rookie here but there are slangs you shouldn't use, especially to older people'.

Titi nodded slowly. 'Now I understand. When I get home, I will apologise properly'.

The use of language can be very complex because it is unique to every environment. It is the principal method of communication that fosters human interaction, so when you move to a new place, knowing how to interact is essential. As a returnee, you cannot survive in isolation. This is why you need to establish a good rapport with people around you by learning the nuances of their language.

When I moved to Nigeria, I didn't have any friends because I didn't grow up here, but I had a cousin who had moved to Nigeria before I did. Although due to my upbringing, I was aware of some of the nuances of Nigerian culture, like how to communicate respectfully, there was still so much I needed to learn about language.

Contrary to what people think, living in the U.K doesn't mean you have to throw away all there is about your culture. My parents raised me to understand this in my early years and it stuck with me. For instance, in the U.K I could greet my colleague or a non-Nigerian with a handshake, but not a Nigerian—an elderly Nigerian, at that. When greeting them, I either kneel or give a slight bow.

Notwithstanding, there is more to communicating with a Nigerian, more so when you are in their environment. If you are not mindful, you may offend people unknowingly.

So, I will be sharing some dos and don'ts regarding what to say as a newbie. It will help you figure out how to communicate with Nigerians in your new environment without stepping on people's toes. If you don't consider this, trust me, you will make more enemies than friends.

If you have friends or relatives in Nigeria who can put you through, it is not everything they will tell you. They can share the bits they know, but it is better to learn from a similar experience rather than create a negative one. Creating a bad experience is undoubtedly a hard way to learn.

From my experience, understanding the way to communicate is crucial to your survival because it will help you build long-lasting relationships. Nigeria has its complexity in language, especially how it is interpreted. This is why Africans in the diaspora need to understand that it is not about what you say, but how you say it and who is listening.

You might say the right things, but how you present it could make it obnoxious.

In Titi's case, she felt she said the right thing. Still, her statement was potentially rude in the Nigerian setting, and she further compounded the situation by walking out. Just the act of walking out, when an older person is talking, is considered condescending and can provoke an adverse reaction.

I come from a typical Yoruba family, and I know how important gestures are to Nigerians. When greeting an elderly person, your gesture is important. I don't extend a handshake; I either kneel or slightly bow.

A handshake here in Nigeria is a big slap to an elderly person. Your words may be polite, but the gesture is degrading

This may be uncomfortable for you as a returnee because this is different from what you are used to. It can be frustrating sometimes, but you have to adjust. Don't throw caution into the wind like Titi under the cloak of *it doesn't matter*, because it does. Never forget the fact that you are in a new environment, with new people and new culture. If you want them to understand you, you have to understand them too.

Words you consider harmless may be regarded as condescending in a typical Nigerian society and interpreted as an insult. Not every Nigerian has been abroad; they may not understand your colloquial language, and in most cases, it can be misconstrued.

The first step to minding your language in a new territory is to observe your environment; know what works for it. Listen more than you speak and learn new things that will aid your adaptability.

***

Another communication snag for returnees is the use of comparison. After relocating to a new environment, there is a feeling of dissatisfaction we often experience when we see the new approach to things, especially when the new method brings no improvement. Well, in such a state, it can be very patronising to state the obvious and complain incessantly while comparing your current environment to where you are coming from. Those words you utter may just be expressions of displeasure to you, but people around you are repetitively reminded of their problems in ways they don't want to.

Therefore, if you are planning to relocate to a new environment like Lagos, or you probably moved recently and you are still trying to figure out how the new environment works, one helpful tip you should not ignore is minding the use of comparison lingos. Comparison lingos are verbalised pent-up frustrations.

When I relocated to Lagos, I discovered so many exasperating things and sometimes wished I could just screech at the top of my voice. But that wouldn't change anything. As I joined the Lagos system, I now understand how Lagosians feel when they listen to returnees relentlessly complain about the environment. They feel disrespected and alienated in their space.

I also understand the plights of returnees, owing to my experience of frustration. I know how irksome it felt adjusting to the strange lifestyle. Today, I simply advise returnees to embrace the organised chaos of Lagos life. Even if the way things are done here is alien to you, don't articulate your frustration using comparison lingos. Steer clear of adding phrases like, *back in the States...; in London, we don't do this...; only in Nigeria...* in your speech. Such lingos will only put you in a disadvantaged position.

In my few years living in Nigeria, I fully understand that lamenting these downsides gratifies the problem. In case you don't know, Nigerians are fully aware of their problems. They recognise the bad roads, the dilapidated infrastructures, the erratic power supply, and they expect that before relocating, you would have made appropriate findings. When you move, don't keep complaining about what is going wrong without appreciating the good things available.

For returnees already entangled in the web of comparison, try to desist from the act by dwelling on positive things even in seemingly dire situations. Life is not a bed of fresh roses, and no country is perfect, not even England, but the ability to navigate your way around makes all the difference. I have learnt to avoid the urge to rant about pent-up frustration or compare Nigeria to England. The lifestyle is different, the culture is different, the language is foreign, and I have accepted the uniqueness of the megacity, Lagos.

Of course, I complain about inadequate services or manners when I encounter such. Still, I do so in a non-aggressive or assertive way, deliberately avoiding narratives like, 'back in the States, we don't do this', 'you only find this in Nigeria', 'in London we don't do this'. If there is a need to correct or adjust anything, I do so without those condensing slangs.

I will always advise prospective returnees to change the way they think about things they cannot fix. Sincerely, that comparison is bound to happen because of the sorry state of things here. Still, you should not let it overwhelm you because there are good things about Nigeria that you will enjoy.
Despite these experiences, I have learnt that comparison will never solve anything. I have tried it and it didn't work, so I stopped focusing on the negatives. Don't get me wrong. I am not saying these challenges do not exist; I only choose to stick to things I can control.

For Africans in the diaspora planning to make that big move back home, remember that there will be many negative issues in Nigeria clamouring for your attention. Still, you have the choice to yield or focus on the few positive ones.

One of the things you will quickly realise on your return is how much the western world has shaped your thinking and orientation on a myriad of issues. This dichotomy between you and your new environment will soon become evident in the conversations you have with friends, family and strangers in the coming months. Living in the western world, or even in other countries around the globe exposes you to a different mindset. Exposure to a different way of thinking is often a positive thing. Yet, it can also be a burden to bear when you find yourself a lone wolf amongst a crowd that believes the opposite of what you believe.

When you return, it is tempting to loudly share your unique ideas or opinions with everyone around you. Many returnees have made the mistake of seeking to convince people on issues with their arguments and oratory skills. In their excitement to share their knowledge, they blurt out their ideas without paying attention to the norms of their new environment.

In the western world, speaking your mind is seen as a great attribute, as it shows you are bold and assertive. But in a patriarchal society like Nigeria, speaking your mind connotes something totally different, and often conjures up negative stereotypes and perceptions of the outspoken returnee in question.

After having to learn from experience when I first moved to Nigeria, my advice is that you sometimes learn to dance to the tune of the people you now live with. Of course, there will be mistakes made at the beginning as you adjust to your new environment. That's where having an open mind comes as an advantage. In the process, though, you will learn to know when to talk and when to remain silent, as well as knowing the right thing to do and say in these situations.

Knowing when to speak in public may seem like such a small thing. But people could easily label you 'the young lady, or young man, who is very rude', simply because you failed to greet them appropriately on one occasion. Being labelled and misjudged, however, is kind of a big thing here. Trust me, you don't want to be known as a rude person who doesn't respect their elders and who is too outspoken for their own good.

Having a good reputation and maintaining it is an extremely important ingredient to successfully adapting to your new culture, especially if you are an entrepreneur trying to create or grow your brand.

Being known and seen in a negative light is something you want to avoid as much as you can because instead of drawing people close to you, you end up getting people riled up and irritated with you. This can work against you in terms of finding a community, networking, and growing your brand. Bad news travel, gossip spreads, and people you have never met may hear things about you that are not true.

The sad thing is that you might know a lot about a subject of discussion, but because of the way you have presented yourself and the perspective people have of you, your narratives take a different turn. But you quickly learn that there is just something about learning to speak at the right time. It is not every time you disagree with something being said that you should voice it out. Sometimes, you just need to let it go. At other times, you wait for the right opportunity to present itself for a one-on-one discussion with the individual in question. At this moment, it is okay to express your understanding of the way you think and where you are coming from, and also allow them to explain where they are coming from. Then, you can share why you think and see things differently.

Another thing to watch out for is easily taking offence to what you see as stupid and backward thinking. The truth is that you will see some very strange and weird things that will get you riled up, but you have to be diplomatic and take the high road and choose not to express your ill feelings in public. Speaking your mind about certain issues in public is not a way to tackle things; all it will do is taint your name and reputation instead.

Dealing with people in your new environment requires maturity and sensitivity on your part. A great way to get people on your side is not to attack their opinions or how they think, instead, slowly train them to think differently about issues and situations. This will require a lot of patience on your part.

However, if the people you are trying to influence with your opinions and thoughts sense that you are attacking them, they will become defensive and more resistant to whatever you are saying to them—whether it benefits them or not. Using that method will defeat the whole purpose you are trying to achieve. The best way to get what you want is by understanding where people are coming from. When I realised this, it was a game-changer for me.

In Nigeria, there are still a lot of people who have archaic thought processes that affect women more than men. As a woman, single or married, returning to Nigeria, you need to be aware of how patriarchal the culture is in so many ways.

You will encounter people who still believe that a woman's place is at home—in the kitchen. If you have lived in the western world for most of your life like I did, it can be a shocking experience to come home and hear all the outdated norms. Sometimes, you might be tempted to scream when you hear such statements. Imagine a young person who has been working since they were 16 years old being told that her place is in the house.

However, that tactic would not work as people are very much stuck in their ways. This means the onus is on you to take the time to explain yourself differently. I wish you could scream and kick down doors and let people know how stupid their thoughts are, but that would not work in a society like Nigeria where men are still seen as demigods.

This underestimation of women also happens in the office board rooms and offices where women are meant to be seen, not heard. When you make your presence known in the office, be prepared to hear the mutterings around why you're so 'out there'. In Nigerian parlance, it's called being an ITK (*I too know*). Sometimes, people will be surprised to hear that you are the leader, and they may try to undermine you and underestimate the value of what you have to say and bring to the conversations.

Sometimes, you also have to watch out for how people treat you differently than your male colleagues. They will try to be casual with you when talking to you verbally and through written communication, instead of maintaining formal and professional decorum.

You will have to nip this in the bud as quickly as you discover it. It's best to set the tone from the start by being professional when dealing with men, either as colleagues or clients. Of course, you want to set the tone in a very informal way that is not off-putting but firm at the same time. When it comes to communicating with people of the opposite gender, you need to watch out for and stay clear of the blurred lines that might occur when you don't set boundaries from the start.

In the end, remember that you are of value and worth, and you can stand up and speak up for yourself in a polite way while setting boundaries.

■ Chapter 4 ■

MAKE CONNECTIONS
TO AVOID DISCONNECTION

There is usually excitement in the air when one first moves to a new country. It's like seeing the world with new and fresh insights. However, there is one thing that often mars the experience if care is not taken, and that is the emptiness one feels without the connections they had back in their former home.

As humans, we are social creatures, and over time we build connections with people who share the same history or experiences with us. We thrive by belonging to a community in whatever form that may take. The problem then arises when, for whatever reason, we bid goodbye to our communities to set up a new home in another country. We become like trees that have been transplanted from their original place of planting.

This means that for you to take root successfully in your new environment, there is a need to interact and build strong relationships. Interaction is designed as a necessity for your survival, and like every other thing you need in your new environment, social interaction is important too. The more interactions you make with people, the easier it becomes for you to settle in and enjoy your new home. Of course, it's not about the number of friends you have but the quality of those new relationships you develop that enriches your life.

In your new environment as a returnee, the first relationship you make will reverberate on your subsequent relationships throughout your stay in your new home. Your first connection is mutually rewarding because, through that one friend, you get access to a ton of other friends—that's how you start building a network of people.

Good networks are built on relationships; you need people's help to succeed in life. Networking doesn't only happen in the comfort of your home. Anything that gets you out of the house is an opportunity to meet new people and admit a new member to your circle of friends. Instead of chatting on the internet, go for a drink or join a book club. If you like sports, register at a gym or join a tennis club.

Do something that gets you out of your house. The person at the tennis club may just be the ticket to your new job, and the guy at the restaurant may be the supplier of the product you need to kickstart your business, but you will never know if you don't start up a conversation with them. While you are at it, try to know them better and add value to their lives.

***

Making connections leads you to have conversations with people, and conversations open doors to opportunities. One remarkable conversation I had that nudged me forward in my career when I came to Nigeria was with Tola Odunsi, whom I was introduced to by my cousin.

The conversation I had with him was my catalyst into the entertainment industry. It was an opportunity I leveraged, which landed me my first salaried job at Storm Records (A prominent record label at that time). The job gave me other opportunities to travel the world, learn leadership skills, and meet CEOs and other high-ups in the entertainment industry.

Even when the job ended, the relationship I built with Tola Odunsi gave me another opportunity to work with him again at Urban Vision. All these opportunities I got at the beginning of my career were products of the first conversation I had with him. My cousin introduced me to him, but if I hadn't sustained the conversation and created a lasting impression, I wouldn't have built a working relationship with him.

Engaging and sustaining a conversation is a skill you need to learn to interact and build a better relationship with people. While conversing with your new neighbour or someone you just met, practice active listening. Unless you are focused and pay rapt attention, you may not understand the underlying message, which you can then use to your advantage and sustain a meaningful conversation.

Interacting with people may come easy and natural for some, but for others, it may not be so. Irrespective of this, building a healthy relationship with people is a process that requires commitment and effort from your end. Even if your excuse is that you are introverted, be conscious of the fact that making a connection with people is a necessity for your new life.

Typically, networking begins with a casual conversation, which could be a telephone conversation, social media interaction, or one-on-one meetings. You can start up a conversation by paying someone a compliment—tell them something you like about them politely and smile. Sure, it may be uncomfortable for some moments, but the feeling would give way when you get to know each other. While interacting, be sincere with the information you divulge; get to know people for who they are and be eager to help the same way you seek help.

As a returnee, broaden your perspective on building networking, and you will realise that every day offers you the opportunity to meet and connect with someone. Networking can happen anywhere since it's about talking to people and making a genuine connection; it isn't limited to a particular environment. Make the most use of those random encounters. You never can tell the benefits that lie within them.

Whatever you do, please don't say no to opportunities to try something new. Remember to see this as an adventure. Yes, it may not be what you are used to, but you never know who you might meet at the events you get to attend.

In the first few months, you will probably get invited to many places, as your friends and family members may want to show you off. Please seize these opportunities because a time will come when they may not have the time for you like they did when you first returned.

There are some myths and misconceptions about networking that leave people confused, but also stop them from taking advantage of opportunities that can easily make a difference in their new lives as they adjust to settling down in a new environment.

One misconception people have about networking is that it is a waste of time. Maybe we think this way because we often see networking events as formal and boring events, so we stay away. The truth is, you are probably doing it all wrong. Networking is not an activity that produces instant results the moment you dive into it. Also, many of us have the mistaken view that networking is supposed to produce immediate results, so we are heartbroken when we don't get our anticipated results; we quickly fold our hands and surrender in defeat. However, networking does not work that way. The appropriate attitude is to see it as some sort of investment, which takes time now but yields tremendous benefits in the future.

Sadly, we live in a fast-paced society where people are not patient enough and are always looking for shortcuts. To be really good at networking requires time and strategy.

Another misconception about networking that stops people in their tracks, especially those who are introverted, is that   networking is best for those who are extroverted and naturally outgoing. But networking is a skill that anyone who puts in the time and effort can learn and then go on to reap the rewards—whether introverted or extroverted.

One more misconception that plays with people's heads and messes with their efforts with networking is the belief that networking is best done only amongst those in your close circle of friends or network. That couldn't be further from the truth. Imagine just limiting yourself to a small river to catch fish when there are bigger places you can sail to and cast your net to capture even bigger resources. Networking can be done anywhere: at a place of worship, in grocery stores, or at your niece's or children's school play. Anywhere you meet with people is a good place to network.

By looking at networking with new eyes and looking beyond the obvious places and our comfort zones, we widen and deepen our horizons, which in turn gives us fresh perspectives and ideas that can open new doors and opportunities to us, which ultimately expands not only our world but our world views and how we see and experience the world.

***

Networking is about meeting the right people. There is nothing at all lacking in this perspective, but of course, one thing you probably may not know is that networking is not just about who you know but those who know you too.

In as much as you need assistance, understand that networking isn't about begging for favours or money. Don't make the mistake of being a nuisance around people by demanding favours too frequently. Even if there is a need for such a request, get to know them first, ensure that a firm relationship has been established. People who take advantage of other people are tagged 'users'. Don't be a user! As much as you are allowed to know and meet people, don't take it for granted. You don't get to play smart on people in Lagos and get away with it; once they realise your biased intentions, you won't last long.

Meeting people is only the first step, but leaving a lasting impression is the second. While the former is all about knowing people, the latter is about getting them to know you.

When you see networking as a tool to build a healthy relationship, you will develop authenticity and add value to people you meet.

Creating an impact doesn't have to be offering services or products. It can be in the eloquence of your speech, the way you articulate, your gesture, your manner of approach, and the way you relate and sustain conversations.

Adding value to people is not always about selling products. You will be surprised at the many ways in which you can help someone. You may be the solution they need. It is easier for someone to warm up to you, associate, and relate with you when they find you useful and helpful. Networking is a marketing technique that spills into other aspects of your life.

Networking comes with its own set of challenges, and I encountered them while marketing my products (*Blinx lashes*). It wasn't easy at first introducing my business to a market I was not familiar with. I encountered people who didn't want to help me. I met people who were too busy to attend to my needs. I also met downright rude people. Those were awkward moments for me, but I also met nice, friendly, and accommodating people. In summary, I experienced the good, the bad, and the ugly.

You are likely to encounter such challenges as a returnee when building your new network. You will meet people you don't like and people who don't like you. They might find you lousy; you might find them too dull, depending on which end of the stick you are holding.

One important thing you should know, despite all challenges, is that you can't be friends with everyone—that's part of the process; don't take it personally or dwell on it either. You need to accept the risk that comes with networking; otherwise, there is no gain.

***

As a returnee in Nigeria, you need to understand the intricacies of networking in a new environment. Lagos may look small, but when it comes to people, it's in no way small. Networking is everything; don't underestimate the importance of the people around you. You need people's assistance to get by in one way or the other. You need assistance, no doubt, but sometimes big names don't always equal big opportunities. So, before taking advantage of people, think twice. Networking is not a one-way ticket; both parties gain from it.

Everything you want can only be accomplished through the help of people. Go out, meet people and build relationships that are mutual and beneficial. A network is only good if it's maintained.

Your relationships need personal attention; devote time and effort to sustain the relationships you've built. Pick up the phone and chat, get out to events, make sure you are easy to socialise with, wear a smile, and be approachable.

■ Chapter 5 ■

JOIN THE HUSTLE BUT DON'T BURST YOUR BUBBLE

Every day on the busy streets of big African cities, people come out in crowds to make a living. They wake up at the crack of dawn to hustle, and you can feel their enthusiasm to work—their energy is almost unlike that of Western countries.

Despite the challenges in Nigeria and other African countries, you can tell that there is exuberance and restlessness amongst the people that spark up the cities. It's no surprise then that moving back home is an exciting time for most returnees, that and the amazing sense of community that comes with the African continent.

One of the perks of living in Nigeria or anywhere else on the African continent is the feeling of community.

Whether it's celebrating a milestone, grieving the loss of a loved one, or just living life, you can always expect the steady support of a community.

And with the astute seeing Africa as an emerging market with a lot to offer the world, an increasing number of people in the diaspora see enough reason to make the move back to their roots, like you probably are too. They are leaving their well-defined lives and relationships abroad to restart their lives in a familiar yet new place.

Before you hastily pack your bags and leave the life you've built behind, I advise you to put things into careful consideration. Truly, Africa is all these things: energetic, communal, and emerging, but you need to understand some things before your move. You need to educate yourself as extensively as possible and put plans in place to manage the many factors that could distract you from thriving in your new environment.

Making Wrong Assumptions

Having lived or studied abroad, returnees develop a sense of independence, and they rightly feel a sense of pride for successfully adapting to a different culture.

But when they move back home, they assume wrongly that they will not need the doggedness and energy that they needed to thrive abroad. They underestimate the demands of their new environment, believing that as returnees, opportunities should be easy to come by.

While it is true that there are a lot of opportunities, you need to be savvy to get them. The truth is that a lot has changed since you left home, so you can't expect to fit in as soon   as you return. For so many reasons, making the wrong assumptions can prove costly. In your ignorance, you could sign problematic business partnerships or even make acquaintances who threaten the success of your return—this can mean anything from people who make you burn through your savings or get on the wrong side of the law.

Although you may have lived your formative years in Nigeria, you have to understand that there are nuances that have evolved since your last time home—nuances that you might not be able to pick up on in conversations, which could make a big difference in how you negotiate your new environment.

Another way you can be making the wrong assumption is in your attitude towards work.

Generally, your status as a returnee does give you an advantage, but you will be wrong to believe that it is a VIP ticket to the job market or business funding. Moving back to your home country is not a licence to be slack at work. On the contrary, you might need to work even harder to prove yourself credible to the people seeking to hire you or do business with you.

The best attitude to have once you return is to observe and learn, as if you are an immigrant coming into a new country. When you are an immigrant, you automatically have the mindset to work hard to adapt and thrive in your new environment. That mindset should still be the same when returning home. While you might be returning with your degree, which ordinarily should open doors of employment for you, a degree is sadly no longer sufficient to get the job you desire or deserve. It is no longer enough to depend on just your qualifications. This can be frustrating, but instead of sulking, you have the choice of seeing this as an opportunity to sell yourself to your new audience and show that you have a lot more to offer. One way to do that is to exhibit an excellent work ethic and resilience.

Nothing is the Same

I'll start by presenting you with an all-too-familiar situation. Say you have this actor whom you love and through a wild stroke of luck, you find yourself face to face with him. At that moment, you feel like a child who just discovered ice cream. At some point, the star-struck mirage starts to clear from your eyes and you start noticing little differences:

He's a bit shorter than he appears on screen. His hair is dark brown and not as deep-black as you had thought. The little differences keep popping out till it dawns on you that he's not the exact depiction of his on-screen personality.

It's the same scenario for a person who is just returning to Lagos, Nigeria. You have built a perception of what working in Nigeria would feel like in your mind, most of which would have come from social media, movies and other third-party sources. While this might prove helpful, it doesn't prepare you for the shock of real life.

My advice? Prepare to be overwhelmed by feelings and experiences—ones that you may recognise due to a prior introduction via a third party. To be on the safe side, mentally exaggerate whatever experiences that may have been relayed to you.

Take, for example, the traffic situation you'd very likely encounter during most of your working life in Lagos. Nothing describes being in Lagos traffic better than the experience itself. It is that way with most of the other experiences you'll encounter while working in Lagos.

The most you can do is prepare to be shocked. Whatever information you've gathered over time will not be a replica of what you'll experience. Notions you might have to do away with; things you'll have to unlearn, and for every day, a practical aspect to the theoretical part of what you've learnt.

As hard as these may seem, it is vital for your navigation of the waters of working in Lagos. It's better to be prepared than have it come upon you unexpectedly. However, the good news is, you won't have to do this for an extended period. Before you can blink, your tenure for the Lagos school of life would have wrapped up, with you passing in flying colours.

Nothing good comes easy, and this is just another one of those tests that leave you a better person. Every city probably says it, but for Lagos, it is the real deal that anyone who survives here can survive anywhere—in this case, in any work environment.

For those gearing up to experience Lagos soon, you'll realise that Lagos is different in real life, but you'll be just fine.

Beware of the Over Excitement in the Air

The temptation to relax, take it easy, and work less is often worsened by the excitement surrounding one's return home. Having that much excitement is customary and expected. The problem is when this exciting atmosphere becomes a distraction. In all the excitement of reuniting with loved ones, it is easy to be carried away by the merriment that will happen. After all, your family and friends want to celebrate your return.

There will also be occasions that people will invite you to, and while it is a good way to establish connections, you must not lose sight of your main goals. It is okay to say 'no' if you don't want to party; you don't have to be at all the events you are invited to. And if you decide to go to these events, be strategic about networking and connecting with people who will become valuable contacts for your personal and professional growth.

The problem with letting the excitement of your return cloud your mind is that it dulls your senses. You fail to see that the people you are partying with are already settled into life at home, leaving you at a disadvantage because settling back home will take a while.

Hustle Makes Lagos Bubble

Lagos may be small, but not its population; that's why living in Lagos is such a unique experience. The traffic, the noise, the nightlife, the energy, and the aggressiveness of the city are just part of its charm. Lagos is Lagos. But for a lot of people who move to Lagos after living in other cities for most of their life, know this, the hustle in Lagos is real.

Hard work is not a myth but a fact. However, you need to add some smart work to your hard work. There are almost half a million people who relocated to Lagos, not just from abroad, but from other cities in Nigeria too, to make a better life and hustle their way to success.

This demands an extraordinary level of alertness and wisdom from new arrivals in the city. You don't want to get scammed by desperate people trying to make it at all costs, so, be careful.

Lagos is like a double edge sword—the enthusiasm and agility may seem inspiring at times, and sometimes it may also be scandalous or likely both at once. The best way to survive in a city like this is to add smart work to your hard work.

It's just simply how Lagos is. But this doesn't happen just in Lagos. I realise it happens in other large and populated cities in the world too.

The Moment Your Move Back Home Becomes Final

When you return, you might find yourself falling into a familiar rhythm, i.e. how you did things during your past visits. In doing that, you stand the risk of treating your move as a holiday, and this can be a challenge for your relocation.

But as it starts to dawn on you that you have returned home to stay, you might start noticing the hard work involved in the process. Part of what that means is finding your way around amenities that you no longer have, which you used to have at your disposal. This can be discouraging. You might even find yourself rethinking your decision to move. When you hit this part of your return, I want you to know that you have reached a milestone in your move back home, and you're not the only one who feels that way.

One way to motivate yourself past the discouragement is to remember that you have done it before and not only survived but also thrived. If you thrive in one country, you can thrive in another, regardless of the limitations it presents. You just need to find new ways to achieve what you want. For many returnees, that means experimenting to find the right approach for your new living situation. It might be tempting to hold on too firmly to how you did things in the United States or the United Kingdom, or whatever developed country you were in.

Different situations require different methods, and just because one method worked for you when you lived abroad does not mean it will work elsewhere.

You need to be flexible when dealing with issues and concerns when you are settling into the hustle and bustle of what is your new abode.

The truth is that you need to have a reorientation when settling back into life at home. Just like you had an orientation when you moved abroad, you need it when returning home. That way, you are less taken aback by the culture shock you will inevitably experience in your new environment.

In some cases, it's reverse culture shock you need to be mindful of; that can be both mentally and emotionally draining. You may have nursed a perfect picture of home in your mind, only to find that things have changed drastically and you don't fit in as well as you once did. Now, you have to relearn how to fit in again, and for returnees who felt like outsiders in another country, this can be both isolating and confusing when they experience it in their home country.

In the end, no one can tell you what your experiences will be when you move back home. Some have a great experience, while others don't. The best you can do is prepare as well as you can and learn everything you can about your home country (or wherever you are relocating to), no matter how familiar it is to you.

■ Chapter 6 ■

EMPLOYEE OR EMPLOYER?

One of the most significant predicaments you might face as a returnee is deciding which path to tread, to generate income in your new environment. While there are many options, it can still be a hassle to find the best route for your journey. How does one decide to either start a business on their own or choose a career where things are more predictable?

I cannot give you a set answer, but I can tell you that no one size fits everyone. The answer lies in your court, with individuals having to figure out what works for them. The truth is, some returnees are better off starting a business, and others are better off with a job.

To make the right decision about your earnings, you need to think through your options carefully and match them with your professional and financial goals. Even then, you may find yourself wavering between both. I am one of those people who can do several things well. I'm an astute entrepreneur and a professional, so I can thrive anywhere. People like me find it difficult to make that choice because we don't want our diverse strengths to waste. I understand, but chasing both professional and entrepreneurial options isn't the best option for a returnee, especially within the first few months of your arrival in your new environment. You need to understand your environment before merging a business with a job as a returnee and thriving at both.

When I moved back to Nigeria, I knew I wanted to start a business, even though I still intended to build my career, which I eventually did after settling and understanding the environment and the game.

My focus and attention were on my business in those early months of my return. So, it was easy to grow it to a point where it was profitable. However, the moment I shifted my attention and started to work on more than my business, it wasn't long before I couldn't meet the demands of the market and of course, consumers' attention then shifted elsewhere. I hadn't planned efficiently.

It was not that my business couldn't work, but it didn't work because my effort and attention were split into several directions. It would have been successful if I had the resources to employ people to look after my business while I face other things.

Of course, nobody sets out on a project without thinking of the future success we hope comes with the new job or business in our new environment. Success is a subjective term, so our opinion may differ. My definition of business success isn't a side hustle or salary support. I view a successful business as an instrument that can create self-sustaining, long-term financial security.

But suppose you want to have a successful career and run a little side business. In that case, you have to be mindful of the chaotic nature of city life—I'm speaking from my experience.

If you would start a one-man business as a returnee, focus on that first and build it. If you have tried it for a while and are not making headway, you can pivot to get a job. If it's a job you decide to start with, you can go that route.

My point is, focusing on one dream at a time gives you better insight into what works best for you. Then, you can carve a niche for yourself or choose another suitable option.

***

The journey to either start a business or look for a job isn't a smooth ride. You need to be prepared for a few bumps along the road.

An essential criterion before embarking on a journey is having a destination in mind. Knowing where one is going in terms of your career or business means first having an idea of what you want to accomplish. And then having a career or business plan to see these ideas come to life.

The same principle is true for those brave enough to start a business in Nigeria. There must be a solid plan in place. You have no excuse for not having a clear goal in mind because even nomads have a destination they want to get their cows to (a fresh pasture to graze).

Your business plan is the blueprint for your business; it gives you a sense of direction and serves as a guide. You don't want to start a business and watch your resources get flushed down the drain.

Starting a business in Lagos is not for the faint-hearted, as the reality of starting a company cannot be captured fully with a few words and figures on paper. No matter how promising your business idea is, you need to prepare yourself for an eventful ride because the factors that helped businesses to succeed where you are coming from might be deficient or worse, absent in Nigeria.

In other words, you must be ready for things to go wrong. I know you're very optimistic about the success of your business. However, when you enter the market with your product or service, you're still testing its market viability.

When you think of starting a profitable business, there is nothing wrong with getting a job when you first arrive in Nigeria to earn a living and gather the income needed for your future venture, especially when you lack the required capital to start your business. You must understand that starting a new business venture requires money.

If getting a job is not an option for you or being an entrepreneur is a dream you want to pursue immediately upon your return, it's essential to make necessary plans to secure the capital needed. You also need to make a note and a list of possible sources of funds. Will it be family and friends providing financial support? If not, where are you going to get the funds? Your savings, or getting loans from financial institutions? These are all options to weigh as you think about creating your own business.

Now that you have sorted out the finances, finding the right location for your business is another essential factor in having a successful business in Lagos. If it's an online business you decide to venture into, you may not necessarily need a physical location. But to build a successful online business, you will have to build trust. Lagosians won't trust you with their money so quickly. For starters, you still need to acquire an office space and run both an offline and online business simultaneously. That would be more efficient if you are looking to build a big company. People would be able to trace your business to an actual location.

When looking for a space, carry out your research correctly. For instance, a hair salon will thrive in a place close to the market or a residential area, not a place close to an airport or factories.

There are many highbrow business areas in Lagos, just ask questions, conduct research, and you will get the best place that suits your business.

Once you have taken care of the location, the next step is to figure out how the business will operate, including staffing concerns. However, while making plans on staffing, operation, and all others, it is essential to be flexible and open to changes. Sometimes, even the ideas you think are new already exist, especially in a place like Lagos—the commercial hub of Nigeria. Even at that, you can still carve a niche for your business, make a profit, and grow.

Personally, Lagos has taught me how to run a business successfully. And if you're moving here, it can do the same for you, provided you listen, watch, learn, and act accordingly. What you need to discover are effective strategies to reach your target audience.

Taking cognisance that you are in a new environment, you need the experience to drive sales and appeal to people's needs. Since the result of the business is to make profit, you need to know the right strategy. One strategy is to learn the business language of Lagos, which is pidgin. Even if you don't speak or understand local dialects, you can interact with everyone in pidgin; they are more likely to understand that.

Like I also emphasised in the previous chapter, networking is vital in business, especially in Lagos. Don't take the relationships you've built for granted; it will help you grow your business.

Another thing I'll tell you is to build your brand identity as you grow. Your brand's identity should reflect your business values and culture. It's what makes your business attract your customers. In building your brand's identity, consider the tangible and intangible aspects of business, such as your logo, brand name, business registration, taglines, social media, and customer services. You also need to optimise social media.

Almost every business is online these days, so you need to have an active social media account to advertise your business and reach a wider audience. These days, a lot of businesses operate online. There are so many advantages that come with doing business online. The first is the low cost of doing business on many of these platforms; you can choose to host your business for next to nothing. Doing business online also gives you room to expand your market beyond a physical location, and by partnering with logistics companies, you can get your goods to your customers. Another bonus is efficiently marketing your business to your target audience through free advertisement or paid sponsorship and adverts.

***

If you are among the lucky few to secure a job before relocating, that's great, if not, don't be discouraged. It can be a bit tiring trying to book a job in advance before relocating. Your intent to get a job in advance is good, but sometimes it may not happen, and this is not because there are no opportunities.

Lagos has a myriad of opportunities yet to be harnessed, but sometimes, you need to be available to access them. By being available, I mean being present for interviews. Thankfully, technology has eliminated the need for that. When I was relocating, it was difficult to scout for opportunities online because the internet hadn't gained as much popularity as it has today.

To access job opportunities that are a good fit for your competencies and requirements, you need to know where to search and be prepared to talk to people. Ask your family, friends, cousins, and relatives for job vacancies. They have been in Nigeria long enough to know more about the system than you do. If you think you can get it all on the internet, you might miss out on a lot. There are some key roles you might be qualified for that are not thrown open to the public. Be willing to drop off your CV and talk to people about it.

A well-paying job in Nigeria may not match up to a well-paying job where you're coming from. The first job I landed didn't come with an attractive salary compared to what I was earning in the UK, but I needed the experience and relationship. From that one job, I had access to tons of others.

In your quest for a job opportunity as a returnee, be open-minded. Your first offer may not be advantageous monetarily, but as a newbie, don't place more value on money than you do on relationships and experience. Connections and expertise will help you work your way faster to the pinnacle of your career. Even if you have a benchmark for your salary or position, be ready to make compromises and get through the door first.

Regardless of the position or sector you find yourself in, always bring your A-game and not just your certificate. Employers expect more from you than your certificate. It shouldn't come to you as a surprise; most employers look for highly efficient and competent people—people with strong work ethics are more valuable to an organisation.

As a returnee, a strong work ethic is a culture you've probably developed while living abroad, so why not use it to your advantage?

***

I have worked real jobs throughout my stay in Nigeria. I had job roles such as head of A&R, brand consultant, marketing and advertising, etc. Most of the opportunities I got came from relationships I built. I didn't keep quiet when I needed a job. Don't pride yourself in being a loner; ask questions when you need to.

You will struggle to secure a job in Lagos if you think you can figure it all out alone, but when you speak up, you will gain access to potentially life-changing opportunities.

Before I decided to focus on my career as a lawyer, my last job was at an international restaurant franchise in Victoria Island. It was a full-time job as the Head of Marketing and Events. A friend mentioned it casually, and though I did not study marketing, I seized the opportunity. I realised the creative industry had given me a lot of experience in this field, so I went for the interview.

My degree didn't get me most jobs. Relationships, experiences, and strong work ethic did. I proved myself capable enough to utilise the opportunities I was given, and it earned me people's trust and valuable relationships.

If you ask me which is better between a business and a job, based on my experience, I will say it depends on your preference. Ultimately, your happiness matters when making this decision because it will determine where you are going, who you will meet, and what you will do. The most important thing is that you get long-term financial stability.

BEFORE YOU MOVE TO NIGERIA

■ Chapter 7 ■

THE ART OF
FLEXIBLE PLANNING

Titi smiled as she sat at a cosy cafe in Lekki, Lagos, reflecting on her return to Nigeria 12 months prior. Chatting with one of her new friends gave her a chance to think back to all she had gone through moving back to Lagos.

As she discussed with Nkechi, Titi found herself laughing at the disparity in their experiences. It was far from what she first imagined when she lived in the United States.

The images she had concocted in her mind proved to be very different in reality. Many of her well-laid plans had crumbled. She had gotten all worked up and depressed when, six months after the move, she found herself in a financial conundrum.

Thankfully though, having a good friend like Nkechi, who had already gone through the process, was life-saving. Titi quickly picked up on the fact that she had to be flexible with her planning. Immediately she realised that little nugget, she began to see options she never considered before.

*****

When you live abroad, your perception of your home takes on a deep, nuanced meaning. You begin to long for home and hunger for things that connect you to your home, like the local news or cuisine. The longer you are away, the more you get the craving to move back, and your short visits only cement the need for a permanent return.

Some people get this longing to move back and begin to act on the urge. They include young people who have spent most of their lives abroad and have been bitten by the bug to return home after visiting for a Christmas holiday. The bustling and entrepreneurial spirit in these bubbling places speaks volumes to them, and they want some of that action. They see lots of potentials and feel drawn to be a part of what is taking place.

Another set is people who are established in their careers and have been posted back home to help either start a branch or run the company.

The third set is those who have spent most of their working years abroad and want to retire to a place where they have people who care for them.

These different individuals return home with similar goals in mind—to settle in happily. However, their path to getting there will be different. The mistake returnees often make is expecting everyone's experience to be the same.

Moving back home must be considered with careful planning. To be successful in this journey of resettlement, you need to become a pro at this game, and this means doing things differently when it comes to planning. It means thinking outside the box and being flexible with certain decisions.

Sometimes, it's easy to get stuck in the ways you did things while living abroad. However, that only leads to more frustration because the system in countries like Nigeria, Ghana, or Kenya is not going to be anything like the UK, the US, or any non-African country you might be returning from. Expecting things to go the way you want just because that's what you are used to, is a recipe for disaster.

Before moving, make necessary plans. Things are better when you have a plan, but in those moments when things change drastically, you should be able to make necessary modifications.

Being too rigid with your plans can make you lose out on opportunities that may not tick all the boxes at first, but can open doors for wonderful things to come. Having an open mind is the beginning of wisdom; it enables you to see things that you might otherwise miss if you stay too focused on your original plans.

Plans are great but they sometimes go wrong; either we miss something or something out of the blues happens; that's why you have to be flexible in your planning. Whatever can go wrong will probably go wrong. I know this doesn't sound positive, but if you think about it, not all the things you plan always go right. And the people who have the hardest time with life are the ones who flip out when things go wrong.

The art of flexible planning simply means having a good plan in place, yet knowing how to monitor and adjust it for challenges, risks, as well as making improvements when needed. Often, people make fixed plans, and when they can't follow through, they give up.

You may be thinking, 'What's the point of having a plan if you cannot stick to your plans anyway', like putting together a daily plan on things you want to accomplish but not being able to execute them due to unforeseen circumstances.

It's important to know that sometimes, things beyond your influence may happen in your life. If you want to be flexible, then accept what you can't change and focus on the ones you can change. If you follow this rule, you will be able to focus your energy on the right things.

What I do is prioritise. For instance, when scouting for apartments, you probably have your specification—things you require in the house, the environment you want it located, etc. What happens if you don't get everything in one place? In that case, what you need to do is get your list of specifications and group them in order of priorities. Pick the house that ticks all your priority boxes.

You may not get all things done on your list, and that's ok, but you can reshuffle your list. At the end of the day, check out all you've done and re-prioritise. Re-adopt a new plan to keep you on track.

There are so many unknowns out there, but flexible planning happens such that you can say to yourself, 'Even though I laid out a plan, if something goes wrong, I can make another plan. I don't have to flip out or fall. I can be adaptive in responding to things and move on'.

You can only rise again when you are flexible enough to try again. No one plans to fail, so when you're taking a step towards a goal and you fail, you don't give up, you try again. Trying again wasn't part of the plan, but if flexibility is, then you would be ready to give it another shot.

You can't determine when your plans fail, especially in a new environment, but you can decide which way you want to go when that happens. For instance, whenever things don't go as I have planned, I look around and say, 'Though it didn't work, I have to work it out'.

There is always a solution; you just have to figure out how it works. Good planning gives you the flexibility to pivot if your original plans go awry. Just because things didn't go as planned initially doesn't mean you've failed. Instead, flexible planning gives you more options to adapt to unexpected roadblocks.

Typically, having an open mind allows you to see the world the way it is, rather than how you think. This flexibility in your thinking will enable you to adapt easily to your new environment and truly thrive.

How can you do this?
- Scope out the new territory

Where will you live? This is a very important part of the puzzle you need to figure out. Knowing your base gives you the freedom to explore and find out the possibilities you can enjoy in your new location.

These surveillance trips to see suitable living spaces give you the data you need before making a decision as huge as moving back. They are good opportunities for you to look for the kind of jobs available or what businesses you can do. It is also a good time to look at different locations and see what housing options are available and how much planning you need to do towards it.

If you are a parent, you want to also look at the type of schools available and the cost of sending your children to the best schools.

One key question to ask is, 'What kind of social amenities are available for you and your family?'

Remember that everyone's story is not the same. In practical terms, this means that if everyone you know is moving back and choosing to live in highbrow areas like Lekki, you don't have to do the same. If you do choose Lekki, it should be after you have looked at other options and decided that it is the best option for your unique situation.

Another tip is to keep your eyes and ears open because important information can come from different and unexpected places. It could be the cab driver who drives you around, a stranger at the bank, or someone you meet randomly at a party. I once got a job offer sitting by a poolside—it happened because I was open to discussing my business ideas and job search in an open and informal way.

It is important that you share what you are looking for so others can point you in the right direction.

Once you have gathered all the data, then you can start making concrete plans for your move back. But it is important to have it at the back of your mind that circumstances can change, especially if you're moving to a place like Nigeria where structures are not as stable. So, even when planning, have alternative options just in case your original plan does not take shape.

- Set the initial stage

Finances are a big determinant of what options are available to you. When you are single and have age on your side, the relocation process might be easier for you than a married person with a family. A young, single person might have the luxury of moving before getting a job or starting a business. However, someone with a family may need to have a job offer or a business before moving their family.

When it comes to moving one's family, it's probably a good idea that either the father or mother moves first to test the situation before moving everyone else.

Whatever plans you have, you can set the ball rolling first. You don't have to wait until things are perfect to make the move. Sometimes, it is after you have set the stage that things become even clearer.

●   Review strategies at intervals

After your move, it is important to review your plans occasionally. This gives you a chance to see what has worked and reflect on some of the things you could do differently. You can always change direction and find a path that fits you and your unique situation. Having an open mind will enable you to see the different options available to you.

Remember, it's not necessarily how you start but how well you adapt and thrive that will matter in the long run.

▪ Chapter 8 ▪
FINDING YOUR COMMUNITY

Music was playing in the background as people mingled and interacted with others in the spacious resort in Accra. While there was meat on the grill, some people snacked on the variety of food spread out on the table. Titi was with Nkechi and some others, playfully splashing around in the pool as they played fun games like Marco Polo.

This was a get-together that Titi had been looking forward to for some time. These people were the community she relied on to keep her shoulders high in an environment that could be intense and stressful at times. After a few months of searching for a community when she first moved to Lagos, she had been delighted to find like-minded people on Instagram. It was a travelling agency that offered members a chance to make trips as a group, both locally and internationally.

Titi's eyes lit up as she looked at all the pictures of past events and trips. This was something she longed to do. She has always had a sense of adventure; she quickly sent a DM to the group and signed up for the next upcoming event, a trip to Badagry.

On that trip to Badagry, Titi learnt the history of Lagos. She soon found herself chatting with many of the group members outside of the group. She enjoyed their company.

Since that first trip to Badagry, Titi had gone on other trips, within and outside Lagos with the group. She now considered them as beloved friends; she always left their gatherings refreshed and ready to take on the world.

***

Settling down in a new place requires courage, an adventurous spirit, and finding your community. Finding your community in your new environment may be smooth as peanut butter or as challenging as scaling the top of Mountain Kilimanjaro, depending on how you view the process—essentially your mindset. Are you a glass-half-full, or half-empty kind of person? Your perspective compels and colours your experiences.

Don't get me wrong, finding your community can be challenging, but how you view those challenges determines how you scale through.

We all have different quirks—things that are unique and vital to us, but we are social beings, and we thrive when we have a safe place where we can bond over things that matter to us. As a returnee, part of your goal is to find your community or communities.

Why? Moving and settling down in a new environment is not only physically draining, but also often emotionally and psychologically tasking. Hanging out with people who understand you is not only inspiring, but it also refuels you. It encourages you to keep going when you naturally want to fold up and collapse on your bed.

After the initial excitement of moving to Nigeria, there is the likelihood that there will be a break when things come to a standstill. In these moments, you will begin to realise that the grass is not always greener on the other side. You will start to desire a reprieve, and the urge to go back to your normal life grows stronger with time.

However, before jumping into the steps you can take to find your community, let's look at some of the reasons why you need a community as a returnee.

- The need to fit in

After all the initial merriment surrounding your return, people will go back to their everyday lives, and you will be left to sort and organise your life. This is where finding your community plays a significant role. No matter how often you visited Nigeria in the past, things have changed, and you need to adapt and figure out the best way to assimilate.

If you are an extrovert, expanding your network might be a lot easier. But for an introvert, that might sound like bloody murder. However, fitting into a group is essential, not only for your physical and mental well-being but also for opening doors to opportunities that you otherwise wouldn't have access to.

- Adapting and dealing with culture shock

Reverse culture shock is a thing, but it's not often acknowledged or spoken about as much as its counterpart. People take for granted the shock that could result from moving back to Nigeria, your cultural home, which can be a huge culture shock if you have lived outside the country for many years. People assume you can just come back and pick up all the lifestyles particular to Nigerians living in Nigeria with ease. That couldn't be farther from the truth.

One has to wade through so many cultural differences when settling down in a new place. Just because you share the same language or come from the same village or town does not mean that you still subscribe to all the tenets of the culture.

The process of wading through these differences can be painful, especially if you are not surrounded by people who understand and get your position on the different issues you will encounter as you slowly settle into life in Nigeria.

There are many aspects of the Nigerian culture and experience that can be jarring to people just returning, which could prove dangerous to their mental and physical health in the long run without a support system

Instead of seeing the world from a place of optimism, you will soon find that your worldview gets coloured by your mixed feelings, which can negatively impact your lifestyle and relationships in your new home.

● Finding and managing relationships
The fastest way to settle into a new place is to find people who love and support you, and, most importantly, understand you. Often, we make the mistake of assuming that our biological families are the best people to fill our needs for belonging when we make a move. Don't get it twisted; While your biological family is essential, it might be necessary for you to expand your network beyond your family because there are some things you will go through that your family would not understand or help you with; Sometimes, they may not completely understand you, especially if they have never been in your situation

No matter what your relationship status is—whether single, married or dating—you need to figure out how to manage your current relationship or find one if available and ready to date in your new environment.

Suppose you are married or in a relationship and you moved back as a couple, it is helpful to find a community you can be a part of while also finding your own space and community as an individual. That way, you can adjust to the new environment and make friends as a couple and as individuals, thereby ensuring a healthy relationship. Moving to a new environment can be challenging to a relationship. This can happen when the couple is not on the same page. A good example is if one is struggling to fit in while the other is a social butterfly. Hence, you need to find a community that meets your needs while also finding a community you both enjoy as a couple. Sharing a community is fantastic because you get to share some of the same passions and tastes that could help build a stronger relationship.

For those who are single, finding your community can also open the doors for you to find your next boyfriend or girlfriend.

The truth is that no matter how self-sufficient you are, you need a community; the absence of one leaves you vulnerable, disconnected, and sometimes lonely.

We have looked into why returnees need to find communities that help them blossom in their new home. The big question remains, 'How then do returnees find their people and communities, especially if they have never lived in Nigeria before?'

Below are some tips that could help you in your adventures of finding your people.

● Go out and explore

There are always diverse communities within a central community. However, we are always quick to put everything in the same category. In our ignorance, it is easier to give in to your frustration and think that you are all alone and no one gets you.

If you stay in your bubble, you most likely will be clueless about the fantastic world around you. So, the first thing you need to do is to begin exploring. Exploring allows you to see what's on the ground and helps you figure out where you need to be when it comes to finding a community.

It does not matter if you grew up in Nigeria or elsewhere, as long as you have been away from Nigeria for a substantial time. You need to be aware that you are moving into a new environment, no matter how familiar it may seem. Sometimes, we are quick to overestimate our adaptability in fitting into what we might consider our old stomping grounds. The best mindset is to start from scratch.

On a personal level, that's what I had to do—I only really knew one person when I moved to Nigeria, which was helpful. But I did go out and explore on my own. The first community I plugged right into was the beauty/fashion community, as strange as that may sound. Joining this community helped me meet friends and go out to the different occasions that come with being part of the beauty community.

I loved makeup and beauty, and I was always keeping my eyes open for information. Thankfully, I got a lot of answers online. I also kept up to date with what was happening within Nigeria's beauty and fashion industry by reading articles online and in print. The wonderful thing about the internet is there was all this information about upcoming events being organised by different players in the industry—there were all these friendly little hangouts. This period was before Instagram became popular, so people had to meet physically.

It was so much fun because there were these beautifully put together events, like fashion fairs and beauty and cosmetic fairs. These events offered an excellent opportunity to connect with interested people.

You would find events and people that connected with the things that you liked and enjoyed. And you would just start going to where the people you followed went. Thankfully, because of social media, people want to show where they are going to be—Influencers can quickly inform you of all the hip events taking place. You know those Facebook and now Instagram posts where people state, 'Guys, catch me at this event or function at the weekend', or make statements like, 'Oh, I am happy to be supporting this particular brand, and they are having an event'.

As I started going to more and more of these events, I met people of the same passion. These people then became my friends, and soon we started hanging out of the original settings.

It wasn't long before my new friends would invite me out, saying, 'let's go grab a bite to eat'. From these extra outings, conversations started to extend to other things outside the passion of beauty and fashion that had brought us together.

That's what you will find once you let go of your fears and start hanging out with people who share the same passion and value as you. The more you hang with people in your community, the more you start to see the other things you have in common with these people.

Before long, your new friends will introduce you to other friends both within and outside your current circle. 'Come and meet my good friends' will become commonplace and open you to new friendships as you try to hang out with these new acquaintances. In this way, you are now exposed to another group of people, thus expanding your social circle.

It is incredible how you can begin to mingle with people from subgroups within the larger community through one community.

- **Do the research and put yourself out there**

Now, a word of caution, while you should always be open to exploration, you still need to think about your safety whenever an opportunity arises. Of course, joining every subgroup you are invited to may not always work for you, and that's okay. Not every community is your community, but be open to trying at least once, because sometimes you might find deep friendships in places you least expect.

You also have to be careful when you attend these events. If you feel uncomfortable after the first outing with a particular community, please put your health and safety first and limit your exposure to that specific space. For example, if you know you succumb to peer pressure easily, you need to stay away from people who are too adventurous. Also, if you are not a heavy drinker, and a few drinks can quickly knock you off your feet, or you don't have the discipline not to drink more than a glass, then maybe joining a community where members often attend cocktail events or hang out at bars may not be a good fit for you.

However, if you are strong in your convictions and don't easily bow to peer pressure, you have the freedom to be more adventurous while remaining true to your beliefs and convictions.

I don't drink alcohol, but that doesn't stop me from attending wine tasting events; this may be difficult for some people. If you find yourself in a group and there is something that goes beyond your personal preferences, feel free to walk away. You will find other communities that suit your interest.

- Be diverse in the communities you join

It is essential to know that spending quality time with people in one setting does not mean you will fit into all the subgroups. It is perfectly normal to only follow friends to certain occasions. You don't have to attend every event with them.

However, there are people with whom you relate so well that you want to keep hanging out with. These are your core group of friends, and finding them might require a bit of trial and error—you have to be adventurous in doing this.

For a start, you may need to honour a lot of invitations, then become more specific about which outing works best for you. You can then put aside the excursions you don't enjoy.

For instance, some people don't like clubbing; others don't enjoy concerts; while others don't like seminars or conferences. You will only know what you want if you are willing to experiment and, in the end, going through all these experiments is well worth the effort.

Trying different things sometimes opens your eyes to the things you do like. If you are interested in sports, there are sporting activities like tennis, swimming, and joining a gym that allow you to account with a diverse number of people. If you are a foodie, there are communities you can join.

Sometimes, you meet people at activities you don't like. Sometimes, the things you don't enjoy doing can connect you with people who share your dislike for the activity and find something you both want together. Take, for example, the person who likes Jazz music and does not like clubbing, but goes to the club one time and meets someone who also does not like the music playing in the club and likes jazz music. Now you have found a friend with similar taste and can connect in attractive ways, such as attending jazz events together.

Other Tips

When finding your community or communities, an essential skill needed is the ability to listen well and keep your ears on the ground. Some things you learn during conversations around you could help and give you access, like when someone says they need help with an activity. Find out what is going on around you and plug yourself into a community.

The next tip is to volunteer and contribute to efforts and causes around you when opportunities arise. Because by offering your services, you open doors for yourself. Due to this exposure, now people know you can do certain things and begin to see you as a trusted contributor to the community.

If you are passionate or have knowledge about a specific issue or subject, do not be afraid to share it with others. Sometimes, we have a lot of wealth within us, but we are too scared to share it because we feel that people might not get what we are about when it comes to our skills or passion. But you never know who is watching and paying attention. Meanwhile, your core audience is out there, waiting for you to share your knowledge and experiences through writing, audio, and videos. The remarkable thing is that with social media, there are so many platforms these days that you can take advantage of, to put yourself and what you do out there. What you put out will draw your desired community to you. What you put out, you will get back.

The next tip is to be vocal about what you do and your passions. People need to know you to find you; they will likely find you the same way you look for them. Therefore, you need to put yourself out there, showing your passions, skills, and talents; be like a billboard, promoting what you want to do or love to do. Stop giving excuses, don't say because you are in a new environment, you don't know what to say, or that you don't know anyone in the industry you are seeking to break into. It's easy to fall into the trap of giving reasons.

For example, you could be interested in graphic designs or video games. Promoting your interests will give people the opportunity to know about you and reach out, thereby, causing new doors to open to you, and before you know it, you will find a group that aligns with your interests.

I was passionate about beauty, and I had a beauty brand when I moved to Nigeria. I would speak about my passion for makeup in the little platform I had, or in the little circles I belonged to. I also went beyond talking and took the effort, then I paid and set up little stalls at the different fairs and events I attended, so you know I was very vocal about it.

By being consistent, the people in these communities could feel my passion for beauty. Before you know it, I started hearing words such as, 'Okay, I know someone who can do this', and I was introduced to some new spaces. One good example was when I wrote articles for the Exquisite Magazine and eventually became their Beauty Editor.

▪ Chapter 9 ▪

TAKE THE TIME TO SMELL THE ROSES

What a journey it has been. I can imagine all the thoughts and questions that have plagued your mind since the thoughts of returning to Nigeria began to swirl around in your brain. From the moment you decided to move back home to Nigeria, I am sure that you have gotten a lot of solicited and unsolicited advice from friends and loved ones.

It can be confusing to have all these pieces of information coming at you from all angles. Often, the advice is coming from people who may not have ever relocated, so you are left wondering how to gauge all these pieces of knowledge about moving back home.

As one who has been in your shoes, I wish I had the information I have compiled and put together in this book to help you be more prepared. In the pages of this book, we have looked at so many facets to consider when relocating back to Nigeria. You might also have loved ones in your ears whispering to you that the challenges you will face may not be worth the move.

The truth is that there will be challenging times that will come once you make a move back home. No book or stories from loved ones can fully prepare you for what you will experience. You will quickly learn that you can't totally rely on other people's perceptions, and you will have to go out there and find out what life in Nigeria has to offer you.

Yes, you will encounter challenges, but what is life without challenges? What is important is that you have the right mindset to tackle those challenges.

Having the right mindset is what will give you fortitude along the way and provide you with the strength to say goodbye to your old life abroad and plunge ahead to a new life in Nigeria. Let's be honest, this is not going to be easy, especially if you have lived abroad for a long time. But hey, in those early days, you will find that you are pumped up with adrenaline and ready for the big move.

But what happens when all that adrenaline and initial excitement fade and you come crashing back to the strange reality that you now live in? Will you just pack up and return to your former life abroad, or will you remain committed to enjoying the beautiful roses despite the thorns?

There will be a variety of experiences you will encounter on your journey back home. You must be aware that not everything will always be rosy, and things will not always go as planned.

When things fail to go according to plan, there will be the temptation to constantly complain or get frustrated and pack up and leave. What you need most during those times of ambiguity is the ability to adapt and be open to new circumstances without losing a beat.

Moving back to Nigeria, you will discover, is a personal journey. Oftentimes , new returnees make the mistake of assuming that their adventure will be just like their friends'. While no two experiences may be the same; there are common challenges returnees would face and have to tackle. That's where this book comes in handy, serving as a practical guide to aid you through this phase of life you've chosen to embark on. My aim with this book is to give you tips as you make your way through every process of moving back.

Moving home is multifaceted, yet many returnees make the mistake of thinking it is a simple return to your roots. However, the truth is moving back to Nigeria is just as complicated as life itself.

Yes, life comes in phases, one of which is your decision to move back home or probably relocate to a new country.

When you see life as a phase, you are more mentally prepared for the journey ahead. Sadly, many people are not fully aware of this nugget. They fail to see that life is in phases and seasons, and that things take time before they grow. So, to be successful, they try to jampack everything into one season of their lives. They think everything should happen immediately.

The reality of moving back to Nigeria is that things will not always go according to plan. Many things will probably go wrong before it comes right in the end. Having the right mindset is what will keep your head above water. A positive attitude will help you to see beyond the present difficulties.

Apart from having the right mindset, if there is one skill that will help you in the long journey ahead, it will be the ability to dust yourself off when you fall off the track. The ability to never give up is a trait that will stand the test of time.

Having both a positive mindset and the ability to get back on your feet will set you free in so many ways. When you have the wrong attitude, it is easy to succumb to the fear of failure. The fear of failure can be demoralising. It can stop you from venturing outside of your comfort zone.

Do you know what's funny? Often, we eventually find fulfilment and joy in the things we were once afraid of. If you are going to thrive in your new home, you have to summon the courage to explore the world around you. The more you open your mind to new experiences, the more you will grow and thrive in your new home.

Moving to another country is stressful, but if you have that mindset of taking everything so seriously, you will not only end up hurting yourself but you'll lose out on so many opportunities that might be outside your frame of reference.

On your journey back home, you will discover how much you will grow and expand your bandwidth once you get out of your head and your current situation and go out of your way to meet with people. Expanding yourself to include others and new experiences is a part of the journey we call life, and you've got to enjoy every bit of the ride. It's not like it will be seamless because there would be potholes and a few bumps of failures here and there.

The unique thing about life is that everyone's path is different. At the time I relocated, I'm sure there were people like me who also made this decision. But not all have stayed back this long. Some may have relocated again to another country after enduring the Nigerian experience for a while; some may have gone back to where they were coming from, and some stayed back as I did.

We are all trying to figure out what works for us, and there are times when we would fail to get it right. What you need to do during those moments is to take a cue from your failure and learn. Try to re-examine things rather than embark on countless trials on things that aren't working.

I mean this in all aspects of life. You can't keep meeting a dead-end and not take a step back to look for another route. If things aren't working in your new environment, try elsewhere.

What's the point, if after hoping things would get better, they don't? Are you staying back because you don't want to be seen as a failure?

Let's take an instance where you are offered your old job back, with an increased salary and position you've always wanted. The only thing that would keep you fighting for your current position here when someone has offered it elsewhere is because you don't want to fail here.

I don't believe your success is tied to a specific location. Assuming victories were genuinely tied to a place, how about people who were forced to relocate due to war or unforeseen circumstances, with all odds stacked against them in their environment, and still became successful?

Listen to yourself properly and determine whether it's time to fight back or take a flight elsewhere. I'm in no way saying give up, pack your bags and leave when it gets tough or when things aren't working. Of course, give your best shot and try again. Still, it would be self-deceptive and unrealistic to keep going in that direction when everything else is pointing the other way.

While it's okay to motivate yourself to get better and keep trying, when the pressure becomes too much, take a bow and do something relaxing.

I know moving into a new home is an experience that very few people describe as fun, but you can throw in some fun; don't take out the fun part in this process. Live a balanced life.

*****

Moving is enough stress itself, adding another in the name of meeting up with expectations. Phew! But that's precisely what many of us do, in one way or another, sometimes without even realising it.

Putting unnecessary pressure on yourself makes things harder and keeps you frantically striving to climb the mountains of expectations you've piled up. You may need to save some of that energy to deal with future stress, especially if you're moving to Lagos, Nigeria.

Not to scare you, Lagos is a great place—one of the closest to (a bubbling city in the UK) if you ask me, but mounting too much pressure on yourself can take out the fun.

Sure, everyone, including you, may be counting on you but just look around you, like take a second look. All you've done is move into a new country. So, ease out some pressure and let out the steam. Have some fun with this relocation process.

If you keep mounting pressure on yourself, you will end up focusing on the wrong things and missing out on the fantastic things that life offers. Like most problems we face in life, pressure is mostly in our minds, and we need to get it out before it gets the best of us. I know we all want to be rich and become billionaires, if it's meant to happen let it happen in due course.

But we all know money doesn't grow on trees abroad, you have to work hard to get it. Though the working conditions are favourable abroad, it still doesn't mean you'll get rich in days or months legitimately except by luck or family heirlooms.

I may not know how your mind works but just think of moving as starting a new project or, better still, getting a new job. You are still trying to get acquainted with the new environment, establish your feet, and get your grip. If you get too pressured, you may even quit before beginning, so just take careful and thoughtful strides as you go along.

Like a new job or project, if you don't love or enjoy what you do, you will get frustrated and keep turning around in circles. Pressure can weigh you down and, over time, knock you out cold with burnout.

Without being too hard on yourself, why not stop the self-sabotage and be your own strongest ally?

There is absolutely nothing wrong with having fun; in fact, it is necessary. A weekly dose is a minimum prescription I recommend for all returnees to keep their minds fresh and live healthily.

Organise your life so that you give time to social engagements like hangouts, parties, lunch dates, etc. Try to do this as much as possible and live a balanced life in your new environment.

***

As I end my thoughts, I will leave you with this advice as a returnee. Don't wait till you've made your millions before visiting your family, especially when you've just relocated to your country. Seriously, should money be the reason why they wouldn't get to see your face after several years?

I don't think so.

For me, that's one good thing about being home. You get to see extended family, grandparents, or bloodline at will. You need to watch out and be wary of being too engrossed in making money and meeting up with certain expectations you've set for yourself. Sometimes, it's just you setting unrealistic expectations for yourself. It's just you pressuring yourself, trying to pile up millions to flaunt around.

At times, all your family and friends want is just to see your face after a long time. Of course, you don't have to visit them empty-handed. Give your family the little you can afford, even if it's just a small monetary gift, food items, household items or gifts.

When you have more, give them more but don't wait till you have millions. Make out time to spend with your folks, including extended families, even if it's only during a festive period, maybe Easter, Christmas, or New Year.

Have fun, hang out, socialise, get to know them better, and enjoy your new home.
Embrace the process in its entirety.

Printed in Great Britain
by Amazon